Joseph Ritson

Ancient Popular Poetry

From Authentic Manuscripts And Old Printed Copies

Joseph Ritson

Ancient Popular Poetry
From Authentic Manuscripts And Old Printed Copies

ISBN/EAN: 9783744695251

Printed in Europe, USA, Canada, Australia, Japan

Cover: Foto ©Thomas Meinert / pixelio.de

More available books at **www.hansebooks.com**

COLLECTANEA ADAMANTÆA.—VI.

Ancient Popular Poetry:

FROM

AUTHENTIC MANUSCRIPTS

AND

OLD PRINTED COPIES.

Edited by

JOSEPH RITSON,

AND

Revised by

EDMUND GOLDSMID, F.R.H.S.

ADORNED WITH CUTS.

VOL. II.

PRIVATELY PRINTED.
EDINBURGH.
1884.

Hazell, Watson, & Viney, Limited, London and Aylesbury.

CONTENTS OF VOL. II.

HOW A MERCHANDE DYD HYS WYFE BETRAY.

I

The story of this ancient poem seems to have appeared in all possible shapes. It is contained in a tract intitled " Penny-wise, pound-foolish ; or a Bristow diamond, set in two rings, and both crack'd. Profitable for married men, pleasant for young men, and a rare example for all good women," London, 1631. 4to. b.l. and is well known, at least in the North, by the old ballad called " The Pennyworth of Wit." It likewise appears, from Langham's Letter, 1575, to have been then in print, under the title of " The Chapman of a Pennyworth of Wit ;" though no edition of that age is now known to exist. The following copy is from a transcript made by the late Mr. Baynes from one of Bp. More's manuscripts in the public library at Cambridge (Ff. 2. 38, or 690), written apparently about the reign of Edward the fourth or Richard the third ; carefully but unnecessarily examined with the original. The poem itself however is indisputably of a greater age, and seems from the language and orthography to be of Scotish, or at least of North country extraction. The fragment of a somewhat different copy, in the same dialect, is contained in a MS. of Henry the 6ths time in the British Museum (Bib. Har. 5396). It has evidently been designed to be sung to the harp.

L YSTENYTH, lordyngys, y you pray,
   How a merchand dyd hys wyfe betray,
Bothe be day and be nyght,
Yf ye wyll herkyn aryght.
Thys songe ys of a merchand of thys cuntre, 5
That had a wyfe feyre and free ;
The marchand had a full gode wyfe,
Sche louyd hym trewly as hur lyfe,
What that euyr he to hur sayde,
Euyr sche helde hur wele apayde :   10
The marchand, that was so gay,
By another woman he lay ;

He boght hur gownys of grete prycc,
Furryd with menyvere and with gryse,
To hur hedd ryall atyre,   15
As any lady myght desyre ;
Hys wyfe, that was so trewe as ston,
He wolde ware no thyng vpon :
That was foly be my fay,
That fayrenes schulde tru loue betray.   20
So hyt happenyd, as he wolde,
The marchand ouer the see he schulde ;
To hys leman ys he gon,
Leue at hur for to tane ;
With clyppyng and with kyssyng swete,   25
When they schulde parte bothe dyd they wepe.
Tyll hys wyfe ys he gon,
Leue at her then hath he tan ;
Dame, he seyde, be goddys are,
Haste any money thou woldyst ware ?   30
Whan y come bezonde the see
That y myzt the bye some ryche drewrè.
Syr, sche seyde, as Cryst me̦ saue,
Ye haue all that euyr y haue ;
Ye schall haue a peny here,   35
As ye ar my trewe fere,
Bye ye me a penyworth of wytt,
And in youre hert kepe wele hyt.
Styll stode the merchand tho,
Lothe he was the peny to forgoo,   40
Certen sothe, as y yow say,
He put hyt in hys purce and yede hys way.
A full gode wynde god hath hym scnde,
Yn Fraunce hyt can hym brynge ;

A full gode schypp arrayed he   45
Wyth marchaundyce and spycerè.
Certen sothe, or he wolde reste,
He boght hys lemman of the beste,
He boght hur bedys, brochys and ryngys,
Nowchys of golde, and many feyre thyngys ;
He boght hur perry to hur hedd,   51
Of safurs and of rubyes redd ;
Hys wyfe, that was so trew as ston,
He wolde ware nothyng vpon :
That was foly be my fay,   55
That fayrenes schulde trew loue betray.
When he had boght all that he wolde,
The marchand ouyr the see he schulde.
The marchandys man to hys mayster dyd speke,
Oure dameys peny let vs not forgete   60
The marchand swore, be seynt Anne,
Zyt was that a lewde bargan,
To bye owre dame a penyworth of wytt,
In all Fraunce y can not fynde hyt.
'An' olde man in the halle stode,   65
The marchandys speche he undurzode ;
The olde man to the marchand can say,
A worde of counsell y yow pray,
And y schall selle yow a penyworth of wyt,
Yf ye take gode hede to hyt :   70
Tell me marchand, be thy lyfe,
Whethyr haste thou a leman or a wyfe ?
Syr, y haue bothe, as haue y reste,
But my paramour loue I beste.

V. 65. And.

Then seyde the olde man, withowten were, 75
Do now as y teche the here ;
When thou comyst ouyr the salte fome,
Olde clothys then do the vpon,
To thy lemman that thou goo,
And telle hur of all thy woo ;   80
Syke sore, do as y the say,
And telle hur all thy gode ys loste away,
Thy schyp ys drownyd in the fom,
And all thy god ys loste the from ;
When thou haste tolde hur soo, 85
Then to thy weddyd wyfe thou go ;
Whedyr helpyth the bettur yn thy nede,
Dwelle with hur, as Cryste the spede.
The marchand seyde, wele must thou fare,
Have here thy peny, y haue my ware. 90
When he come ouer the salte fome,
Olde clothys he dyd hym vpon,
Hys lemman lokyd forthe and on hym see,
And seyde to hur maydyn, how lykyth the?
My love ys comyn fro beyonde the see, 95
Come hedur, and see hym wyth thyn eye.
The maydyn seyde, be my fay,
He ys yn a febull array.
Go down, maydyn, in to the halle,
Yf thou mete the marchand wythalle, 100
And yf he spyrre aftyr me,
Say, thou sawe me wyth non eye ;
Yf he wyll algatys wytt,
Say in my chaumbyr y lye sore syke,

V.V. 79, 80. *These two lines are in the MS. inserted after the four following.*

Out of hyt y may not wynne, 105
To speke wyth none ende of my kynne,
Nother wyth hym nor wyth none other,
Thowe he were myn own brother.
Allas! seyde the maydyn, why sey ye soo?
Thynke how he helpyed yow owt of moche wo.
Fyrst when ye mett, wyth owt lesynge, 111
Youre gode was not worthe xx s.,
Now hyt ys worthe cccc pownde,
Of golde and syluyr that ys rounde;
Gode ys but a lante lone, 115
Some tyme men haue hyt, and some tyme none;
Thogh all hys gode be gon hym froo,
Neuyr forsake hym in hys woo.
Go downe, maydyn, as y bydd the,
Thou schalt no lenger ellys dwelle wyth me.
The maydyn wente in to the halle, 121
There sche met the marchand wythall.
Where ys my lemman? where ys sche?
Why wyll sche not come speke wyth me?
Syr, y do the wele to wytt, 125
Yn hyr chaumbyr sche lyeth full syke,
Out of hyt sche may not wynne,
To speke wyth non ende of hur kynne,
Nother wyth yow nor wyth non other,
Thowe ye were hur owne brother. 130
Maydyn, to my lemman that thou go,
And telle hur my gode ys loste me fro,
My schyp ys drownyd in the fom,
And all my gode ys loste me from;
A gentylman have y slawe, 135
Y dar not abyde the londys lawe;

Pray hur, as sche louyth me dere,
As y have ben to hur a trewe fere,
To kepe me preuy in hur chaumbyr,
That the kyngys baylyes take me neuyr.   140
Into the chaumbyr the maydyn ys goon,
Thys tale sche told hur dame anone.
In to the halle, maydyn, wynde thou downe,
And bydd hym owt of my halle to goon,
Or y schall send in to the towne,   145
And make the kyngys baylyes to come ;
Y swere, be god of grete renown,
Y wyll neuyr harbur the kyngys feloun.
The maydyn wente in to the halle,
And thus sche tolde the merchand alle ;   150
The marchand sawe none other spede,
He toke hys leve and forthe he yede.
Lystenyth, lordyngys, curtes and hende,
For zyt ys the better fytt behynde.

[THE SECOND FIT.]

L YSTENYTH, lordyngys, great and small :
The marchand ys now to hys own halle ;
Of hys comyng hys wyfe was fayne,
Anone sche come hym agayne.
Husbonde, sche seyde, welcome ye be,
How haue ye farde beyonde the see ?   160
Dame, he seyde, be goddys are,
All full febyll hath be my fare ;
All the gode that euer was thyn and myn
Hyt ys loste be seynt Martyn ;

In a storme y was bestadde,   165
Was y neuyr halfe so sore adrad,
Y thanke hyt god, for so y may,
That euyr y skapyd on lyve away ;
My schyp ys drownyd in the fom,
And all my gode ys loste me from ;   170
A gentylman haue y slawe,
I may not abyde the londys lawe ;
I pray the, as thou louest me dere,
As thou art my trewe weddyd fere,
In thy chaumber thou woldest kepe me dern.
Syr, sche seyde, no man schall me warne : 176
Be stylle, husbonde, sygh not so sore,
He that hathe thy gode may sende the more ;
Thowe all thy gode be fro the goo,
I wyll neuyr forsake the in thy woo ;   180
Y schall go to the kyng and to the quene,
And knele before them on my kneen,
There to knele and neuyr to cese,
Tyl of the kyng y haue getyn thy pees :
I can bake, brewe, carde and spynne,   185
My maydenys and y can sylvyr wynne,
Euyr whyll y am thy wyfe,
To maynten the a trewe mannys lyfe.
Certen sothe, as y yow say,
All nyght be hys wyfe he lay,   190
On the morne, or he forthe yede,
He kaste on hym a ryall wede,
And bestrode a full gode stede,
And to hys lemmans hows he yede.
Hys lemman lokyd forthe and on hym see, 195
As he come rydyng ouyr the lee,

Sche put on hur a garment of palle,
And mett the marchand in the halle,
Twyes or thryes, or euyr he wyste,
Trewly sche had hym kyste.   200
Syr, sche seyde, be seynt John,
Ye were neuyr halfe so welcome home.
Sche was a schrewe, as haue y hele,
There sche currayed fauell well.
Dame, he seyde, be seynt John,   205
Zyt ar not we at oon;
Hyt was tolde me beyonde the see,
Thou haste another leman then me,
All the gode that was thyn and myne,
Thou haste geuyn hym, be seynt Martyn. 210
Syr, as Cryste bryng me fro bale,
Sche lyeth falsely that tolde the that tale;
Hyt was thy wyfe, that olde trate,
That neuyr gode worde by me spake;
Were sche dedd (god lene hyt wolde!)   215
Of the haue all my wylle y schulde;
Erly, late, lowde and stylle,
Of the schulde y haue all my wylle:
Ye schall see, so muste y the,
That sche lyeth falsely on me.   220
Sche leyde a canvas on the flore,
Longe and large, styffe and store,
Sche leyde theron, wythowten lyte,
Fyfty schetys waschen whyte,
Pecys of syluyr, masers of golde;   225
The marchand stode hyt to be holde:
He put hyt in a wyde sakk,
And leyde hyt on the hors bakk;

He bad hys chylde go belyue,
And lede thys home to my wyue. 230
The chylde on hys way ys gon,
The marchande come aftyr anon ;
He caste the pakk downe in the flore,
Longe and large, styf and store,
As hyt lay on the grounde, 235
Hyt was wele worthe cccc pownde :
They on dedyn the mouth aryght,
There they sawe a ryall syght.
Syr, sayde hys wyfe, be the rode,
Where had ye all thys ryall gode ? 240
Dame, he seyde, be goddys are,
Here ys thy penyworth of ware ;
Yf thou thynke hyt not wele besett,
Gyf hyt another can be ware hytt bett ;
All thys wyth thy peny boght y, 245
And therfore y gyf hyt the frely ;
Do wyth all what so euyr ye lyste,
I wyll neuyr aske yow accowntys, be Cryste.
The marchandys wyfe to hym can say,
Why come ye home in so febull array ? 250
Then seyde the marchand, sone ageyn,
Wyfe, for to assay the in certeyn ;
For at my lemman was y before,
And sche by me sett lytyll store,
And sche louyd bettyr my gode then me, 255
And so wyfe dydd neuyr ye.
To tell hys wyfe then he began,
All that gode he had takyn fro hys lemman ;
And all was becawse of thy peny,
Therfore y gyf hyt the frely ; 260

And y gyf god a vowe thys howre,
Y wyll neuyr more have paramowre,
But the, myn own derlyng and wyfe,
Wyth the wyll y lede my lyfe.
Thus the marchandys care be gan to kele, 265
He lefte hys folye euery dele,
And leuyd in clennefse and honestè ;
Y pray god that so do we.
God that ys of grete renowne,
Saue all the gode folke of thys towne : 270
Jesu, as thou art heuyn kynge,
To the blys of heuyn owre soules brynge.

HOW THE WISE MAN TAUGHT HIS SON.

This little moral piece, which, for the time wherein it was written, is not inelegant, is given from a manuscript collection in the Harleian library in the British Museum (No. 1596), compiled in the reign of King Henry the sixth. It is not supposed to have been before printed, nor has any other copy of it been met with in manuscript; there is however a striking coincidence of idea in Mr. Gilbert Coopers beautiful elegy intitled "A father's advice to his son," as well as in the old song of "It's good to be merry and wise;" which the more curious reader may consult at his leisure.

LYSTENYTH all, and ze well here
    How the wyse man taght hys son ;
Take gode tent to thys matere,
    And fond to lere yf the con.
Thys song be zonge men was begon,   5
    To make hem tyrsty and stedfast ;
But zarn that is oft tyme yll sponne,
    Euyll hyt comys out at the last.

A wyse man had a fayre chyld,
    Was well of fyftene zere age,   10
That was bothe meke and mylde,
    Fayre of body and uesage ;
Gentyll of kynde and of corage,
    For he schulde be hys fadur eyre ;

Hys fadur thus, yn hys langage,   15
    'Taght' hys sone bothe weyll and fayre :

And sayd, son, kepe thys word yn hart,
    And thenke theron 'tyll' thou be ded ;
Zeyr day thy furst weke,
    Loke thys be don yn ylke stede :   20
Furst se thye god yn forme of brede,*
    And serue hym 'well' for hys godenes,
And afturward, sone, by my rede,
    Go do thy worldys besynes.

Forst, worschyp thy god on a day,   25
    And, sone, thys schall thou haue to 'mede,'
Skyll fully what thou pray,
    He wyll the graunt with outyn drede,
And send the al that thou hast nede,
    As 'far' as meser longyth to strech,   30
This lyfe in mesur that thou lede,
    And of the remlant thou ne rech.

And, sone, thy tong thou kepe also,
    And be not tale wyse be no way,
Thyn owen tonge may be thy fo,   35
    Therfor beware, sone, j the pray,
Where and when, son, thou schalt say,
    And be whom thou spekyst oght ;
For thou may speke a word to day
    That seuen zere thens may be forthozt.   40

V. 16. That.   *V.* 18. thyll.   *V.* 22. wyll.
V. 26. mad.   *V.* 30. for.
      * i. e. *go to mass.*

Therefore, sone, be ware be tyme,
   Desyre no offys for to bere,
For of thy neyborys mawgref,
   Thou most hem bothe dysplese and dere,
Or ellys thy self thou must 'forswere,'   45
   And do not as thyn offys wolde,
And gete the mawgrefe here and there,
   More then thank a thousand fold.

And, sone, yf thou wylt lyf at ese,
   And warme among thy neyburs syt,   50
Lat newefangylnes the plese
   Oftyn to remewe nor to flyt,
For and thou do thou wantys wyt,
   For folys they remewe al to wyde ;
And also, sone, an euyl ' sygne' ys hyt,   55
   A mon that can no wher abyde.

And, sone, of syche thyng j the warne,
   And on my blyssyng take gode hede,
Thou vse neuer the tauerne ;
   And also dysyng j the forbede :   60
For thyse two thyngys, with outyn drede,
   And comon women, as j leue,
Maks zong men euyle to spede,
   And ' falle' yn danger and yn myschefe.

And, sone, the more gode thou hast,   65
   The rather bere the meke and lowe ;
Lagh not mych for that ys wast,
   For folys ben by laghing ' knowe.'

V. 45. for swete.   *V.* 55. sagne.
V. 64. fulle.   *V.* 68. knone.

And, sone, quyte wele that thou owe,
   So that thou be of detts clere ;   70
And thus, my lefe chylde, as j ' trowe,'
   Thou mest the kepe fro davngere.

And loke thou wake not to longe,
   Ne vse not rere soperys to late ;
For, were thy complexion neuyr so strong, 75
   Wyth surfet thou mayst fordo that.
Of late walkyng oftyn debate,
   On nyztys for to syt and drynke ;
Yf thou wylt rule thyn aftate,
   Betyme go to bed and wynke.   80

And, sone, as far furth as thou may,
   On non enquest that thou come,
Nor no fals wytnesse bere away,
   Of no manys mater, all ne sum :
For better the were be defe and dowm, 85
   Then for to be on eny enquest,
That aftyr myzt be vndurnome,
   A trewe man had hys quarel lest.

And, sone, yf thou wylt haue a wyfe,
   Take hur for no couetyse,   90
But loke, sone, sche be the lefe,
   Thou wyfe bywayt and wele awyse,
That sche be gode, honest, and wyse,
   Thof sche be pore take thou no hede,
For sche 'schal' do the more seruys,   95
   Then schall a ryche with owtyn drede.

V. 71. trewe.   *V*. 95. schalt.

For better it is in rest and pes,
  A mes of potage and no more,
Than for to haue a thousand mes,
  With gret dysese and angyr sore.   100
Therfore, sone, thynk on thys lore,
  Yf thou wylt haue a wyfe with ese,
By hur gode set thou no store,
  Thoffe sche wolde the bothe feffe and sesse.

And yf thy wyfe be meke and gode,   105
  And serue the wele and 'plesantly,'
Loke that thou be not so wode,
  To charge hur then to owtragely ;
But then fare with hur esely,
  And cherysch hur for hur gode dede,   110
For thyng ouerdon vnskylfully,
  Makys wrath to grow where ys no nede.

I wyl neyther glos ne 'paynt,'
  But waran the on anodyr syde,
Yf thy wyfe come to make pleynt,   115
  On thy seruandys on any syde,
Be nott to hasty them to chyde,
  Nor wreth the or thou wytt the sothe,
For wemen yn wrethe they can not hyde,
  But sone they reyse a smokei rofe.   120

Nor, sone, be not jelows, j the pray,
  For, and thou falle in jelosye,

V. 106. plesantyl.   *V.* 113. praynt.
V. 118. *The MS. reads* wreth the not, *but the word*
not *is inserted by a different, though very ancient, hand,
which has corrected the poem in other places ; and is
certainly redundant and improper.*

Let not thy wyfe wyt in no way,
  For thou may do no more foly ;
For, and thy wyfe may onys aspye   125
  That thou any thyng hur mystryst,
In dyspyte of thy fantesy,
  To do the wors ys all hur lyst.

Therfore, sone, j byd the
  Wyrche with thy wyfe as reson ys,   130
Thof sche be seruant in degre,
  In som degre she felaw ys.
Laddys that ar bundyn, so haue j blys,
  That can not rewle theyr wyves aryzt,
That makys wemen, so haue j blys,   135
  To do oftyn wrong yn plyzt.

Nor, sone, bete nott thy wyfe j rede,
  For ther yn may no help ' rise,'
Betyng may not stond yn stede,
  But rather make hur ' the to despyse :' 140
Wyth louys awe, sone, thy wyfe chastyse,
  And let fayre wordys be thy zerde ;
Louys awe ys the best gyse,
  My sone, to make thy wyfe aferde.

Nor, sone, thy wyfe thou schalt not chyde,
  Nor calle hur by no vyleus name,   146
For sche that schal ly be thy syde,
  To calle hur fowle yt ys thy schame ;

V 135. *The latter half of this line seems repeated by mistake.*
    V. 138. be.   V. 140. to despyse the

Whan thou thyne owen wyfe wyl dyffaine,
   Wele may anothyr man do so :   150
Sort and fayre men make tame
   Herte and buk and wylde roo.

And, sone, thou pay ryzt wele thy tythe*,
   And pore men of thy gode thou dele ;
And loke, sone, be thy lyfe,   155
   Thou gete thy sowle here sum hele.
Thys werld hyt turnys euyn as a whele,
   All day be day hyt wyl enpayre,
And so, sone, thys worldys wele,
   Hyt faryth but as a chery fare.   160

For all that euyr man doth here,
   Wyth besynesse and trauell bothe,
All ys wythowtyn were,
   For oure mete, drynk, and clothe ;
More getys he not, wythowtyn othe,   165
   Kyng or prynce whether that he be,
Be hym lefe, or be hym loth,
   A pore man has as mych as he.

And many a man here gadrys gode
   All hys lyfe dayes for othyr men,   170
That he may not by the rode,
   Hym self onys ete of an henne ;
But be he doluyn yn hys den,
   Anothyr schal come at hys last ende,
Schal haue hys wyf and catel then,   175
   That he has gadred another schal spende.

---

* *The author, from this and other admonitions, is supposed to have been a parson.*

Therfor, sone, be my counseyle,
  More then ynogh thou neuyr covayt,
Thou ne wost wan deth wyl the assayle,
  Thys werld ys but the fendys bayte.   180

For deth ys, sone, as I trowe,
  The most thyng that certyn ys,
And non so vncerteyn for to knowe,
  As ys the tyme of deth y wys ;
And therfore so thou thynk on thys,   185
  And al that j haue seyd beforn :
And Ihesu ' bryng' vs to hys blys,
  That for us weryd the crowne of thorn.

V. 180.   *The latter part of this stanza seems to be
wanting.*
V. 187. brynd.

THE LIFE AND DEATH

OF

TOM THUMBE.

It is needless to mention the popularity of the following story. Every city, town, village, shop, stall, man, woman, and child, in the kingdom, can bear witness to it. Its antiquity, however, remains to be enquired into, more especially as no very ancient edition of it has been discovered. That which was made use of on the present occasion bears the following title: " Tom Thumbe, his life and death: wherein is declared many maruailous acts of manhood, full of wonder, and strange merriments. Which little knight lived in king Arthurs time, and famous in the court of Great Brittaine. London, printed for John Wright. 1630." It is a small 8vo. in black letter, was given, among many other curious pieces, by Robert Burton, author of the Anatomy of Melancholy, to the Bodleian Library (Seld. Art. L. 79.), and is the oldest copy known to be extant. There is a later edition, likewise in black letter, printed for F. Coles, and others, in Antony à Wood's collection, which has been collated, as has also a different copy, printed for some of the same proprietors, in the editor's possession. All three are ornamented with curious cuts, representing the most memorable incidents of our hero's life. They are likewise divided into chapters by short prose arguments, which, being always unnecessary, and sometimes improper, as occasioning an interruption of the narrative, are here omitted.

In Ben Jonson's Masque of the Fortunate Isles, designed for the Court, on the Twelfth Night,

1626, *Skelton, one of the characters, after mention-ing Elinor Rumming, and others, says*

> *Or you may have come*
> *In,* THOMAS THUMB,
> *IN A PUDDING FAT.*
> *With Doctor Rat.*

Then " *The Antimasque follows: consisting of these twelve persons, Owl-glass, the four Knaves, two Ruffians, Fitz-Ale, and Vapor, Elinor Rum-ming, Mary Ambree, Long Meg of Westminster,* TOM THUMB *and Doctor Rat.*" *

Five years before there had appeared " *The History of Tom Thumbe, the Little, for his small stature surnamed, King Arthurs Dwarfe: Whose Life and aduentures containe many strange and wonderful accidents, published for the delight of merry Time-spenders. Imprinted at London for Tho: Langley,* 1621, (12mo. bl.l.)" *This how-ever was only the common metrical story turned into prose with some foolish additions by R. I.* [*Richard Johnson.*] *The Preface or Introductory Chapter is as follows, being indeed the only part of the book that deserves notice.*

" *My merry Muse begets no Tales of Guy of Warwicke, nor of bould Sir Beuis of Hampton; nor will I trouble my penne with the pleasant glee of Robin Hood, little Iohn, the Fryer and his Marian; nor will I call to minde the lusty Pindar of Wakefield, nor those bold Yeomen of the North,* ADAM BELL, CLEM OF THE CLOUGH, *nor* WILLIAM

---

* *Works, by Whalley, vi.* 195. " *Doctor Rat, the curate,*" *is one of the* Dramatis Personæ *in* " *Gammar Gurtons Needle.*"

OF CLOUDESLY, *those ancient archers of all England, nor shal my story be made of the mad merry
pranckes of Tom of Bethlem, Tom Lincolne, or
Tom a Lin, the Diuels supposed Bastard, nor yet
of Garagantua that monster of men*, but of AN
I.DER TOM A TOM OF MORE ANTIQUITY, a Tom
of a strange making, I meane Little Tom of Wales,
no bigger then a Millers Thumbe, and therefore for
his small stature, surnamed Tom Thumbe. . . . . .
The ANCIENT TALES of Tom Thumbe IN THE OLDE
TIME, haue beene the only reuiuers of drouzy age at
midnight; old and young haue with his Tales
chim'd Mattens till the cocks crow in the morning;
Batchelors and Maides with his Tales haue com-
passed the Christmas fire-blocke, till the Curfew-
Bell rings candle out; the old Shepheard and the
young Plow boy after their dayes labour, haue
carold out a Tale of Tom Thumbe to make them
merry with: and who but little Tom, hath made
long nights seem short, and heauy toyles easie?
Therefore (gentle Reader) considering that old
modest mirth is turnd naked out of doors, while
nimble wit in the great Hall sits vpon a soft
cushion giuing dry bobbes; for which cause I will,
if I can, new cloath him in his former liuery, and
bring him againe into the Chimney Corner, where
now you must imagine me to sit by a good fire,*

---

* *This is scarcely true; the titles of the two last
chapters being, 1. "How Tom Thumbe riding forth to
take the ayre, met with the great Garagantua, and of
the speech that was betweene them." 2. "How Tom
Thumbe after conference had with great Garagantua
returned, and how he met with King Twadle."*

amongst a company of good fellowes ouer a well spic'd Wassel-bowle of Christmas Ale telling of these merry Tales which hereafter follow." This is in the editors possession.

In the panegyric verses (by Michael Drayton and others) upon Tom Coryate and his Crudities, London, 1611, 4to. *our hero is thus introduced, along with a namesake, of whom, unfortunately, we know nothing further* * :

"Tom Thumbe *is dumbe, vntill the pudding creepe,*
" *In which he was intomb'd, then out doth peepe.*
" Tom Piper *is gone out, and mirth bewailes,*
" *He neuer will come in to tell vs tales."*†

We are unable to trace our little hero above half a century further back, when we find him still popular, indeed, but, to our great mortification, in very bad company. "IN OUR CHILDHOOD (*says honest Reginald Scot) our mothers maids haue so terrified vs with an ouglie diuell . . . and haue so fraied vs with bull beggers, spirits, witches, vrchens, elues, hags, fairies, satyrs, pans, faunes, sylens, kit with the cansticke, tritons, centaurs, dwarfes, giants, imps, calcars, coniurors, nymphes, chang-*

---

* This is a mistake: we are all well acquainted with the old lines :
      "Tom, Tom, the Piper's son,
        Stole a pig, and away he run."

† *In a different part of the work we find other charac-ters mentioned, whose story is now, perhaps, irretrievably forgot :*
      I am not now to tell a tale
      Of George a Green, or Iacke a Vale,
        Or yet of Chittiface.

lings, incubus, Robin good-fellow, the spoorne, the mare, the man in the oke, the helle waine, the fiere-drake, the puckle, TOM THOMBE, hob-gobblin, Tom tumbler, boncles, and such other bugs, that we are afraide of our owne shadowes." *

To these researches we shall only add the opinion of that eminent antiquary Mr. Thomas Hearne, that this History, " however looked upon as alto-gether fictitious, yet was CERTAINLY founded upon some AUTHENTICK HISTORY. as being nothing else, originally, but a description of KING EDGAR'S DWARF."* †

IN Arthurs court Tom Thumbe did liue,
   A man of mickle might,
The best of all the table round,
   And eke a doughty knight :

His stature but an inch in height,   5
   Or quarter of a span ;
Then thinke you not this little knight,
   Was prou'd a valiant man ?

His father was a plow-man plaine,
 His mother milkt the cow,   10
But yet the way to get a sonne
 ' This' couple knew not how,

Untill such time this good old man
 To learned Merlin goes,
And there to him his deepe desires 15
 In secret manner showes,

How in his heart he wisht to haue
 A childe, in time to come,
To be his heire, though it might be
 No bigger than his Thumbe.   20

Of which old Merlin thus foretold,
 That he his wish should haue,
And so this sonne of stature small
 The charmer to him gaue.

No blood nor bones in him should be, 25
 In shape and being such,
That men should heare him speake, but not
 His wandring shadow touch :

But so vnseene to goe or come
 Whereas it pleasd him still ;   30
Begot and borne in halfe an houre,
 To fit his fathers will :

V. 12. these.

And in foure minutes grew so fast,
    That he became so tall
As was the plowmans thumbe in height,   35
    And so they did him call

Tom Thumbe, the which the Fayry-Queene
    There gave him to his name,
Who, with her traine of Goblins grim,
    Vnto his christning came.   40

Whereas she cloath'd him richly braue,
    In garments fine and faire,
Which lasted him for many yeares
    In scemely sort to weare.

His hat made of an oaken leafe,   45
    His shirt a spiders web,
Both light and soft for those his limbes
    That were so smally bred ;

His hose and doublet thistle downe,
    Togeather weau'd full fine ;   50
His stockins of an apple greene,
    Made of the outward rine ;

His garters were two little haires,
    Pull'd from his mothers eye,
His bootes and shooes a mouses skin,   55
    There tand most curiously.

Thus, like a lustic gallant, he
    Aduentured forth to goe,
With other children in the streets
    His pretty trickes to show.   60

Where he for counters, pinns, and points,
    And cherry stones did play,
Till he amongst those gamesters young
    Had loste his stocke away.

Yet could he soone renue the same,   65
    When as most nimbly he
Would diue into 'their' cherry-baggs,
    And there ' partaker' be,

Unseene or felt by any one,
    Vntill a scholler shut   70
This nimble youth into a boxe,
    Wherein his pins he put.

Of whom to be reueng'd, he tooke
    (In mirth and pleasant game)
Black pots, and glasses, which he hung   75
    Vpon a bright sunne-beame.

The other boyes to doe the like,
    In pieces broke them quite ;
For which they were most soundly whipt,
    Whereat he laught outright.   80

And so Tom Thumbe restrained was
    From these his sports and play,
And by his mother after that
    Compel'd at home to stay.

V. 67. the.   *V*. 68. a taker.

Whereas about a Christmas time,   85
   His father a hog had kil'd,
And Tom ' would ' see the puddings made,
   ' For fear ' they should be spil'd.

He sate vpon the pudding-boule,
   The candle for to hold ;   90
Of which there is vnto this day
   A pretty pastime told :

For Tom fell in, and could not be
   For euer after found,
For in the blood and batter he   95
   Was strangely lost and drownd.

Where searching long, but all in vaine,
   His mother after that
Into a pudding thrust her sonne,
   Instead of minced fat.   100

Which pudding of the largest size,
   Into the kettle throwne,
Made all the rest to fly thereout,
   As with a whirle-wind blowne.

For so it tumbled vp and downe,   105
   Within the liquor there,
As if the deuill ' had ' been boyld ;
   Such was his mothers feare,

V. 87. to.   *V.* 88. Fear'd that.
     V. 107. had there.

3

That vp she tooke the pudding strait,
 And gaue it at the doore   110
Vnto a tinker, which from thence
 In his blacke budget bore.

But as the tinker climb'd a stile,
 By chance he let a cracke :
Now gip, old knaue, out cride Tom Thumbe,
 There hanging at his backe : 116

At which the tinker gan to run,
 And would no longer stay,
But cast both bag and pudding downe,
 And thence hyed fast away. 120

From which Tom Thumbe got loose at last
 And home return'd againe :
Where he from following dangers long
 In safety did remaine.

Untill such time his mother went 125
 A milking of her kine,
Where Tom vnto a thistle fast
 She linked with a twine.

A thread that helde him to the same,
 For feare the blustring winde 130
Should blow him thence, that so she might
 Her sonne in safety finde.

But marke the hap, a cow came by,
 And vp the thistle eate.
Poore Tom withall, that, as a docke, 135
 Was made the red cowes meate :

Who being mist, his mother went
  Him calling euery where,
Where art thou Tom? where art thou Tom?
  Quoth he, Here mother, here :   140

Within the red cowes belly here,
  Your sonne is swallowed vp.
The which into her feareful heart
  Most carefull dolours put.

Meane while the cowe was troubled much,
  In this her tumbling wombe,   146
And could not rest vntil that she
  Had backward cast Tom Thumbe :

Who all besmeared as he was,
  His mother tooke him vp,   150
To beare him thence, the which poore lad
  She in her pocket put.

Now after this, in sowing time,
  His father would him haue
Into the field to driue his plow,
  And therevpon him gaue   155

A whip made of a barly straw,
  To driue the cattle on :
Where, in a furrow'd land new sowne,
  Poore Tom was lost and gon.

Now by a raven of great strength   160
  Away he thence was borne,
And carried in the carrions beake
  Euen like a graine of corne,

Unto a giants castle top,
　　In which he let him fall,　　　　　　165
Where soone the giant swallowed vp
　　His body, cloathes and all.

But in his belly did Tom Thumbe
　　So great a rumbling make,
That neither day nor night he could　　170
　　The smallest quiet take,

Untill the gyant had him spewd
　　Three miles into the sea,
Whereas a fish soone tooke him vp
　　And bore him thence away.　　　　175

Which lusty fish was after caught
　　And to king Arthur sent,
Where Tom was found, and made his dwarfe,
　　Whereas his dayes he spent

Long time in liuely iollity,　　　　　180
　　Belou'd of all the court,
And none like Tom was then esteem'd
　　Among the noble sort.

Amongst his deedes of courtship done,
　　His highnesse did command,　　　　185
That he should dance a galliard braue
　　Vpon his queenes left hand.

The which he did, and for the same
　　The king his signet gaue,
Which Tom about his middle wore　　　190
　　Long time a girdle braue.

Now after this the king would not
   Abroad for pleasure goe,
But still Tom Thumbe must ride with him,
   Plac't on his saddle-bow.   195

Where on a time when as it rain'd,
   Tom Thumbe most nimbly crept
In at a button hole, where he
   Within his bosome slept.

And being neere his highnesse heart,   200
   He crau'd a wealthy boone,
A liberall gift, the which the king
   Commanded to be done,

For to relieue his fathers wants,
   And mothers, being old ;   205
Which was so much of siluer coyne
   As well his armes could hold.

And so away goes lusty Tom,
   With three pence on his backe,
A heauy burthen, which might make   210
   His wearied limbes to cracke.

So trauelling two dayes and nights,
   With labour and great paine,
He came into the house whereas
   His parents did remaine ;   215

Which was but halfe a mile in space
   From good king Arthurs court,
The which in eight and forty houres
   He went in weary sort.

But comming to his fathers doore,   220
  He there such entrance had
As made his parents both reioice,
  And he thereat was glad.

His mother in her apron tooke
  Her gentle sonne in haste,   225
And by the fier side, within
  A walnut shell, him plac'd:

Whereas they feasted him three dayes
  Vpon a hazell nut,
Whereon he rioted so long   230
  He them to charges put;

And there-vpon grew wonderous sicke,
  Through eating too much meate,
Which was sufficient for a month
  For this great man to eate.   235

But now his businesse call'd him foorth,
  King Arthurs court to see,
Whereas no longer from the same
  He could a stranger be.

But yet a few small April drops,   240
  Which setled in the way,
His long and weary iourney forth
  Did hinder and so stay.

Until his carefull father tooke
  A birding trunke in sport,   245
And with one blast blew this his sonne
  Into king Arthurs court.

Now he with tilts and turnaments
   Was entertained so,
That all the best of Arthurs knights   250
   Did him much pleasure show.

As good Sir Lancelot of the Lake,
   Sir Tristram, and sir Guy ;
Yet none compar'd with braue Tom Thum,
   For knightly chiualry.   255

In honour of which noble day,
   And for his ladies sake,
A challenge in king Arthurs court
   Tom Thumbe did brauely make.

Gainst whom these noble knights did run, 260
   Sir Chinon, and the rest,
Yet still Tom Thumbe with matchles might
   Did beare away the best.

At last sir Lancelot of the Lake
   In manly sort came in,   265
And with this stout and hardy knight
   A battle did begin.

Which made the courtiers all agast,
   For there that valiant man
Through Lancelots steed, before them all, 270
   In nimble manner ran.

Yea horse and all, with speare and shield,
   As hardly he was seene,
But onely by king Arthurs selfe
   And his admired queene,   275

Who from her finger tooke a ring,
　Through which Tom Thumb made way,
Not touching it, in nimble sort,
　As it was done in play.

He likewise cleft the smallest haire   280
　From his faire ladies head,
Not hurting her whose euen hand
　Him lasting honors bred.

Such were his deeds and noble acts
　In Arthurs court there showne,   285
As like in all the world beside
　Was hardly seene or knowne.

Now at these sports he toyld himselfe
　That he a sicknesse tooke,
Through which all manly exercise   290
　He carelesly forsooke.

Where lying on his bed sore sicke,
　King Arthurs doctor came,
With cunning skill, by physicks art,
　To ease and cure the same.   295

His body being so slender small,
　This cunning doctor tooke
A fine prospective glasse, with which
　He did in secret looke

Into his sickened body downe,   300
　And therein saw that Death
Stood ready in his wasted guts
　To sease his vitall breath.

His armes and leggs consum'd as small
   As was a spiders web,   305
Through which his dying houre grew on,
   For all his limbes grew dead.

His face no bigger than an ants,
   Which hardly could be seene :
The losse of which renowned knight   310
   Much grieu'd the king and queene.

And so with peace and quietnesse
   He left this earth below ;
And vp into the Fayry Land
   His ghost did fading goe.   315

Whereas the Fayry Queene receiu'd,
   With heauy mourning cheere,
The body of this valiant knight,
   Whom she esteem'd so deere.

For with her dancing nymphes in greene, 320
   She fetcht him from his bed,
With musicke and sweet melody,
   So soone as life was fled :

For whom king Arthur and his knights
   Full forty daies did mourne ;   325
And, in remembrance of his name
   That was so strangely borne,

He built a tomb of marble gray,
   And yeare by yeare did come
To celebrate the mournefull day,   330
   And buriall of Tom Thum.

Whose fame still liues in England here,
   Amongst the countrey sort ;
Of whom our wiues and children small
   Tell tales of pleasant sport.   335

THE LOVERS QUARREL:

OR,

CUPIDS TRIUMPH.

This "*pleasant History*," which "*may be sung to the tune of Floras Farewell*," is here republished from a copy printed at London for F. Cotes and others, 1677, 12mo. *bl. l.* preserved in the curious and valuable collection of that excellent and most respected antiquary Antony à Wood, in the Ashmolean Museum; compared with another impression, for the same partners, without date, in the editor's possession. The reader will find a different copy of the poem, more in the ballad form, in a Collection of "*Ancient Songs*," published by J. Johnson. Both copies are conjectured to have been modernised, by different persons, from some common original, which has hitherto eluded the vigilance of collectors, but is strongly suspected to have been the composition of an old North country minstrel.

The full title is—"*The Lovers quarrel: or Cupids Triumph: being the pleasant history of Fair Rosamond of Scotland. Being daughter to the lord Arundel, whose love was obtained by the valour of Tommy Pots: who conquered the lord Phenix, and wounded him, and after obtained her to be his wife. Being very delightful to read.*"

OF all the lords in Scotland fair,
    And ladies that been so bright of blee,
There is a noble lady among them all,
    And report of her you shall hear by me.

For of her beauty she is bright,   5
    And of her colour very fair,
She's daughter to lord Arundel,
    Approv'd his parand and his heir.

Ile see this bride, lord Phenix said,
    That lady of so bright a blee,   10
And if I like her countenance well,
    The heir of all my lands she'st be.

But when he came the lady before,
  Before this comely maid came he,
O god thee save, thou lady sweet,   15
  My heir and parand thou shalt be.

Leave off your suit, the lady said,
  As you are a lord of high degree,
You may have ladies enough at home,
  And I have a lord in mine own country ; 20

For I have a lover true of mine own,
  A serving-man of low degree,
One Tommy Pots it is his name,
  My first love, and last that ever shall be.

If that Tom Pots [it] is his name,   25
  I do ken him right verily,
I am able to spend forty pounds a week,
  Where he is not able to spend pounds three.

God give you good of your gold, she said,
  And ever god give you good of your fee, 30
Tom Pots was the first love that ever I had,
  And I do mean him the last to be.

With that lord Phenix soon was mov'd,
  Towards the lady did he threat,
He told her father, and so it was prov'd,   35
  How his daughters mind was set.

O daughter dear, thou art my own,
  The heir of all my lands to be,
Thou shalt be bride to the lord Phenix
  If that thou mean to be heir to me.

O father dear, I am your own,
 And at your command I needs must be,
But bind my body to whom you please,
 My heart, Tom Pots, shall go with thee.

Alas ! the lady her fondness must leave, 45
 And all her foolish wooing lay aside,
The time is come, her friends have appointed,
 That she must be lord Phenix bride.

With that the lady began to weep,
 She knew not well then what to say, 50
How she might lord Phenix deny,
 And escape from marriage quite away.

She call'd unto her little foot-page,
 Saying, I can trust none but thee,
Go carry Tom Pots this letter fair, 55
 And bid him on Guildford-green meet me :

For I must marry against my mind,
 Or in faith well proved it shall be ;
And tell to him I am loving and kind,
 And wishes him this wedding to see. 60

But see that thou note his countenance well,
 And his colour, and shew it to me ;
And go thy way and high thee again,
 And forty shillings I will give thee.

For if he smile now with his lips, 65
 His stomach will give him to laugh at the
Then may I seek another true love, [heart,
 For of Tom Pots small is my part.

But if he blush now in his face,
　　Then in his heart he will sorry be,　　　　70
Then to his vow he hath some grace,
　　And false to him I'le never be.

Away this lacky boy he ran,
　　And a full speed forsooth went he,
Till he came to Strawberry-castle,　　　　75
　　And there Tom Pots came he to see.

He gave him the letter in his hand,
　. Before that he began to read,
He told him plainly by word of mouth,
　　His love was forc'd to be lord Phenix bride. 80

When he look'd on the letter fair,
　　The salt tears blemished his eye,
Says, I cannot read this letter fair,
　　Nor never a word to see or spy.

My little boy be to me true,　　　　　　85
　　Here is five marks I will give thee,
And all these words I must peruse,
　　And tell my lady this from me :

By faith and troth she is my own,
　　By some part of promise, so it's to be found, 90
Lord Phœnix shall not have her night nor day,
　　Except he can win her with his own hand.

On Guildford-green I will her meet,
　　Say that I wish her for me to pray,
For there I'le lose my life so sweet,　　　　95
　　Or else the wedding I mean to stay.

Away this lackey· boy he ran,
  Then as fast as he could hie,
The lady she met him two miles of the way,
  Says, why hast thou staid so long, my boy? 100

My little boy, thou art but young,
  It gives me at heart thou'l mock and scorn,
Ile not believe thee by word of mouth,
  Unless on this book thou wilt be sworn.

Now by this book, the boy did say,   105
  And Jesus Christ be as true to me,
Tom Pots could not read the letter fair,
  Nor never a word to spy or see.

He says, by faith and troth you are his own,
  By some part of promise, so it's to be found, 110
Lord Phenix shall not have you night nor day,
  Except he win you with his own hand.

On Guildford-green he will you meet,
  He wishes you for him to pray,
For there he'l lose his life so sweet,   115
  Or else the wedding he means to stay.

If this be true, my little boy,
  These tidings which thou tellest to me,
Forty shillings I did thee promise,
  Here is ten pounds I will give thee.   120

My maidens all, the lady said,
  That ever wish me well to prove,
Now let us all kneel down and pray,
  That Tommy Pots may win his love.

If it be his fortune the better to win,   125
    As I pray to Christ in trinity,
Ile make him the flower of all his kin,
    For the young lord Arundel he shall be.

THE SECOND PART.

LET's leave talking of this lady fair,
    In prayers full good where she may be, 130
Now let us talk of Tommy Pots,
    To his lord and master for aid went he.

But when he came lord Jockey before,
    He kneeled lowly on his knee,
What news? what news? thou Tommy Pots, 135
    Thou art so full of courtesie.

What tydings? what tydings? thou Tommy Pots,
    Thou art so full of courtesie;
Thou hast slain some of thy fellows fair,
    Or wrought to me some villany.   140

I have slain none of my fellows fair,
    Nor wrought to you no villany,
But I have a love in Scotland fair,
    And I fear I shall lose her with poverty.

If you'l not believe me by word of mouth, 145
    But read this letter, and you shall see,
Here by all these suspitious words
    That she her own self hath sent to me.

But when he had read the letter fair,
   Of all the suspitious words in it might be,   150
O Tommy Pots, take thou no care,
   Thou'st never lose her with poverty.

For thou'st have forty pounds a week,
   In gold and silver thou shalt row,
And Harvy town I will give thee,   155
   As long as thou intend'st to wooe.

Thou'st have forty of thy fellows fair,
   And forty horses to go with thee,
Forty of the best spears I have,
   And I myself in thy company.   160

I thank you, master, said Tommy Pots,
   That proffer is too good for me;
But, if Jesus Christ stand on my side,
   My own hands shall set her free.

God be with you, master, said Tommy Pots,   165
   Now Jesus Christ you save and see;
If ever I come alive again,
   Staid the wedding it shall be.

O god be your speed, thou Tommy Pots,
   Thou art well proved for a man,   170
See never a drop of blood thou spil,
   Nor yonder gentleman confound.

See that some truce with him thou take,
   And appoint a place of liberty;
Let him provide him as well as he can,   175
   As well provided thou shalt be.

But when he came to Guildford-green,
  And there had walkt a little aside,
There he was ware of lord Phenix come,
  And lady Rosamond his bride.   180

Away by the bride then Tommy Pots went,
  But never a word to her he did say,
Till he the lord Phenix came before,
  He gave him the right time of the day.

O welcome, welcome, thou Tommy Pots,   185
  Thou serving-man of low degree,
How doth thy lord and master at home,
  And all the ladies in that country?

My lord and master is in good health,
  I trust since that I did him see;   190
Will you walk with me to an out-side,
  Two or three words to talk with me?

You are a noble man, said Tom,
  And born a lord in Scotland free,
You may have ladies enough at home,   195
  And never take my love from me.

Away, away, thou Tommy Pots,
  Thou serving-man stand thou aside;
It is not a serving-man this day,
  That can hinder me of my bride.   200

If I be a serving-man, said Tom,
  And you a lord of high degree,
A spear or two with you I'le run,
  Before I'le lose her cowardly.

Appoint a place, I will thee meet,　　205
　　Appoint a place of liberty,
For there I'le lose my life so sweet,
　　Or else my lady I'le set free.

On Guildford-green I will thee meet,
　　No man nor boy shall come with me.　210
As I am a man, said Tommy Pots,
　　I'le have as few in my company.

And thus staid the marriage was,
　　The bride unmarried went home again,
Then to her maids fast did she laugh,　　215
　　And in her heart she was full fain.

My maidens all, the lady said,
　　That ever wait on me this day,
Now let us all kneel down,
　　And for Tommy Pots let us all pray.　220

If it be his fortune the better to win,
　　As I trust to God in trinity,
Ile make him the flower of all his kin,
　　For the young lord Arundel he shall be.

THE THIRD PART.

WHEN Tom Pots came home again,   225
    To try for his love he had but a week,
For sorrow, god wot, he need not care,
    For four days that he fel sick.

With that his master to him came,   [doubt,
    Says, pray thee, Tom Pots, tell me if thou
Whether thou hast gotten thy gay lady,   231
    Or thou must go thy love without.

O master, yet it is unknown,
    Within these two days well try'd it must be,
He is a lord, I am but a serving man,   235
    I fear I shall lose her with poverty.

I prethee, Tom Pots, get thee on thy feet,
    My former promises kept shall be ;
As I am a lord in Scotland fair,
    Thou'st never lose her with poverty.   240

For thou'st have the half of my lands a year,
    And that will raise thee many a pound,
Before thou shalt out-braved be,
    Thou shalt drop angels with him on the ground.

I thank you, master, said Tommy Pots,   245
    Yet there is one thing of you I would fain,
If that I lose my lady sweet,
    How I'st restore your goods again ?

If that thou win the lady sweet,
   Thou mayst well forth thou shalt pay me, 250
If thou loosest thy lady thou losest enough,
   Thou shalt not pay me one penny.

You have thirty horses in one close,
   You keep them all both frank and free,
Amongst them all there's an old white horse   255
   This day would set my lady free ;

That is an old horse with a cut tail,
   Full sixteen years of age is he ;
If thou wilt lend me that old horse,
   Then could I win her easily.   260

That's a foolish opinion, his master said,
   And a foolish opinion thou tak'st to thee ;
Thou'st have a better then ever he was,
   Though forty pounds more it should cost me.

O your choice horses are wild and tough,   265
   And little they can skill of their train ;
If I be out of my saddle cast,
   They are so wild they'l ne'r be tain.

Thou'st have that horse, his master said,   270
   If that one thing thou wilt me tell ;
Why that horse is better then any other,
   I pray thee Tom Pots shew thou to me.

That horse is old, of stomach bold,
   And well can he skill of his train,   275
If I be out of my saddle cast,
   He'l either stand still, or turn again.

Thou'st have the horse with all my heart,
   And my plate coat of silver free,
An hundred men to stand at thy back,   280
   To fight if he thy master be.

I thank you master, said Tommy Pots,
   That proffer is too good for me,
I would not for ten thousand pounds
   Have man or boy in my company.   285

God be with you, master, said Tommy Pots,
   Now as you are a man of law,
One thing let me crave at your hand,
   Let never a one of my fellows know.

For if that my fellows they did wot,   290
   Or ken of my extremity,
Except you keep them under a lock,
   Behind me I am sure they would not be.

But when he came to Guildford-green,
   He waited hours two or three,   295
There he was ware of lord Phenix come,
   And four men in his company.

You have broken your vow, said Tommy Pots,
   The vow which you did make to me,
You said you would bring neither man nor boy,
   And now has brought more than two or
      three.   301

These are my men, lord Phenix said,
   Which every day do wait on me ;
If any of these dare proffer to strike,
   I'le run my spear through his body.   305

I'le run no race now, said Tommy Pots,
    Except now this may be,
If either of us be slain this day,
    The other shall forgiven be.

I'le make that vow with all my heart,   310
    My men shall bear witness with me ;
And if thou slay me here this day,
    In Scotland worse belov'd thou never shalt be.

They turn'd their horses thrice about,
    To run the race so eagerly ;   315
Lord Phenix he was fierce and stout,
    And ran Tom Pots through the thick o' th'
        thigh.

He bor'd him out of the saddle fair,
    Down to the ground so sorrowfully.
For the loss of my life I do not care,   320
    But for the loss of my fair lady.

Now for the loss of my lady sweet,
    Which once I thought to have been my wife,
I pray thee, lord Phenix, ride not away,
    For with thee I would end my life.   325

Tom Pots was but a serving-man,
    But yet he was a doctor good,
He bound his handkerchief on his wound,
    And with some kind of words he stancht his
        blood *.

---

* i.e. *he made use of a charm for that purpose.*

He leapt into his saddle again,   330
   The blood in his body began to warm,
He mist lord Phenix body fair,
   And ran him through the brawn of the arm :

He bor'd him out of his saddle fair,
   Down to the ground most sorrowfully ;   335
Says, prethee, lord Phenix, rise up and fight,
   Or yield my lady unto me.

Now for to fight I cannot tell,
   And for to fight I am not sure ;
Thou hast run me throw the brawn o' the arm, 340
   That with a spear I may not endure.

Thou'st have the lady with all my heart,
   It was never likely better to prove
With me, or any nobleman else
   That would hinder a poor man of his love. 345

Seeing you say so much, said Tommy Pots,
   I will not seem your butcher to be,
But I will come and stanch your blood,
   If any thing you will give me.

As he did stanch lord Phenix blood,   350
   Lord ! in his heart he did rejoice ;
I'le not take the lady from you thus,
   But of her you'st have another choice.

Here is a lane of two miles long,
   At either end we set will be,   355
The lady shall stand us among,
   Her own choice shall set her free.

If thou'l do so, lord Phenix said,
   To lose her by her own choice it's honesty,
Chuse whether I get her or go her without, 360
   Forty pounds I will give thee.

But when they in that lane was set,
   The wit of a woman for to prove,
By the faith of my body, the lady said,
   Then Tom Pots must needs have his love. 365

Towards Tom Pots the lady did hie,
   To get on behind him hastily ;
Nay stay, nay stay, lord Phenix said,
   Better proved it shall be.

Stay you with your maidens here,   370
   In number fair they are but three ;
Tom Pots and I will go behind yonder wall,
   That one of us two be proved to dye.

But when they came behind the wall,
   The one came not the other nigh,   375
For the lord Phenix had made a vow,
   That with Tom Pots he would never fight.

O give me this choice, lord Phenix said,
   To prove whether true or false she be,
And I will go to the lady fair,   380
   And tell her Tom Pots slain is he.

When he came from behind the wall,
   With his face all bloody as it might be,
O lady sweet, thou art my own,
   For Tom Pots slain is he.   385

Now have I slain him, Tommy Pots,
  And given him deaths wounds two or three ;
O lady sweet, thou art my own,
  Of all loves, wilt thou live with me ?

If thou hast slain him, Tommy Pots,   390
  And given him deaths wounds two or three,
I'le sell the state of my fathers lands,
  But hanged shall lord Phenix be.

With that the lady fell in a swound,
  For a grieved woman, god wot, was she ; 395
Lord Phenix he was ready then,
  To take her up so hastily.

O lady sweet, stand thou on thy feet,
  Tom Pots alive this day may be ;
I'le send for thy father, lord Arundel,   400
  And he and I the wedding will see :

I'le send for thy father, lord Arundel,
  And he and I the wedding will see ;
If he will not maintain you well,
  Both lands and livings you'st have of me. 405

I'le see this wedding, lord Arundel said,
  Of my daughters luck that is so fair,
Seeing the matter will be no better,
  Of all my lands Tom Pots shall be the heir.

With that the lady began for to smile,   410
  For a glad woman, god wot, was she ;
Now all my maids, the lady said,
  Example you may take by me.

But all the ladies of Scotland fair,
  And lasses of England, that well would
    prove,   415
Neither marry for gold nor goods,
  Nor marry for nothing but only love :

For I had a lover true of my own,
  A serving-man of low degree ;
Now from Tom Pots I 'le change his name, 420
  For the young lord Arundel he shall be.

GLOSSARY.

GLOSSARY.

Abraide, *The word* at *seems to be wanting:* At a braide; *at a push; at a start. It may, however, only mean* abroad.

Adrad, *afraid.*

Algatys, *by all means.*

Among, *between.*

Amonge, *at the same time.*

And, *an, if.*

Apayde, *satisfyed, contented.*

Are, Goddys are, *Gods heir or son,* i.e. *Jesus Christ, who is also God himself.*

Array, *dress, clothing.*

Arrayed, *freighted, furnished.*

Assay, assaye, *essay, try; try, prove.*

Assoyld, *absolved.*

A twyn, *asunder.*

Anaunced, *advanced, prefered.*

Auowe, *a vow, an oath.*

Awyse.

Ayenst, *against.*

Bale, *misery, sorrow, evil.*

Bargan, *business, commission.*

Barker, *a tanner, so called from his using bark.*

Bedys, *beads.*

Belyfe, belyue, *immediately.*

Bescro, *beshrew, curse.*

Besett, *laid out, bestowed.*

Bestadde, *situated, placed.*

Bett, *better.* Ware hytt bett, *lay it out to more advantage.*

Bil, *bill, an old English weapon, called a few lines before* "a pollaxe."

Blee, *colour, complexion.*

Blynne, *stop, cease, give over.*

Blythe, blyue, *blithe, with spirit.*

Boltes, *arrows.*

Bor, *born.*

Bord, borde, *jest.*

Borowe, *bail, redeem, become pledges for.*

Bote, *boot, remedy, advantage.*

5

Bowne, *boon, favour.*

Braste, *burst.*

Brede, *bread.*

Bren, brenne, *burn.*

Brent, *burnt.*

Brest, *burst, broke.*

Brochys, *ornamental pins, or buckles, like the Roman* fibulæ, *(with a single prong) for the breast or head-dress.*

Bundyn.

Buske, *busked, addressed, prepared, got ready.*

Bywayt.

Chaste, *chastise, correct.*

Chaunce. Redy the justice for to chaunce. *This whole line seems a non-sensical interpolation.*

Cheke, *choaked.*

Chery fare.

Clennesse, *cleanness, chastity.*

Clerk, *scholar.*

Cleynt, *clung.*

Clyppyng, *embracing.*

Comand, *commanded, ordered.*

Combre, *incumber, be too many for.*

Corage, *heart, spirit, inclination, disposition.*

Curtes, *courteous.*

Dame, *mistress.* Oure dameys peny. *Our mistress's penny.*

Dampned, *condemned.*

Den, *grave.*

Dere, *hurt.*

Dern, *secret.*

Do gladly, *eat heartyly.*

Doluyn, *delved, buryed.*

Dongeon, *prison. The prison in old castles was generally under-ground.*

Dradde, *dreaded, feared.*

Drede, *fear, doubt.*

Drewrè. *The word properly signified love, courtship,* &c. *and hence a love-token, or love-gift; in which sense it is used by Bp. Douglas.*

Drough, *drew.*

Dyd of, *put off.*

Dyd on, *put on.*

Euerechone, everichone, euerychone, *every one.*

Eyre, *heir.*

Eysell, *vinegar.*

Fadur, *father;* his fadur eyre, *his father's heir.*

Fare, *go.*

Fauell, *deceit. See Skelton's* Bowge of Courte. *The meaning of the text is nevertheless still obscure, though it should seem to be the origin of our modern phrase* to curry favour.

Fay, faye, *faith.*

Fayne, *fain, glad.*

Feble, febull, febyll, *poor, wretched, miserable.*

Feche, *fetch.*

Feffe, *enfeof.*

Fere, *wife, husband, lover, friend.*

Fet, *fit, part, canto.*

Feyt, *faith.*

Flyt, *shift.*

Folys, *fools.*

Fom, fome, *sea.*
Fond, *endeavour, try.*
Fone, *foes.*
Forbode, *commandment.*
  Ouer Gods forbode.
  [Præter Dei præceptum
  sit.] q.d. *God forbid.*
  (PERCY.)
Fordo, *undo, ruin, destroy.*
Forth.
Forthoxt, *thought of, re-
membered.*
Forthynketh, *grieveth,
vexeth.*
Fosters, *foresters.*
Fote, *foot.*
Found, *supported, main-
tained.*
Freke, *fellow.*
Froo, *from.*
Fyt, fytt, *fit, part, canto.*
Fytte, *strain.*
God, *goods, merchandize.*
Godamarsey, *a corruption
of* gramercy. *See* gra-
marcy.
Gode, *goods, property.*
Goo, *gone.*
Goon, *go.*
Gramarcy, *thanks,* grand
mercie.
Greece. Hart of Greece.
Gryse, *a species of fur.*
Gyse, *way, manner, method.*
Harowed, *ravaged, ran-
sacked. Christ went
through hell as a con-
queror, and plundered
it of all the souls he
thought worth carrying
off.*
Hatche, *a low or half door.*

Hedur, *hither.*
Hele, *health.*
Hem, *him.*
Hende, *civil, gentle.*
Hente, *take.*
Hes, *his.*
Het, *it.*
Hie, *go, run.*
High, *hye, come, hasten,
return speedily.*
Hight, *was called.*
Honge, *hang, be hanged.*
Howr, *our.*
Howyn, *own.*
Hye, *go.*
Hyght, *promised.*
Hyne, *a* hind *is a servant.*
Kele, *cool.*
Kneen, *knees.*
Kynd, *nature.*
Lagh, *laugh.*
Laghing, *laughing.*
Lante, *lent.*
Launde, *plain, open part
of a forest.*
Leace, *lyes, lying, doubt.*
Leasynge, *lying, falsehood,
doubt.*
Lee, *plain, open field.*
Lefe, *agreeable,* that is the
lefe, *that is so dear to
thee ; whom thou art so
fond of, dear, or beloved.*
Be hym lefe, or be hym
lothe. *Let him like it
or not ; let him be agree-
able or unwilling.*
Leffe, *leave.*
Leman, lemman, *mistress,
concubine, lover, gallant,
paramour.*
Lene, *lend.*

Lenger, *longer.*

Lere, *learn.*

Lesynge, *lying, falsehood.*

Lette, *delay.* Lette not for this, *be not hindered or prevented by what has happened from proceeding.*

Letteth, *let, hinder, prevent.*

Leue, *believe.*

Leuer, *rather, sooner.*

Lewde, *foolish.*

Lightile, *quickly.*

Linde, *the linden or lime tree ; a tree in general.*

Lith, *incline, attend.*

Lordeyne, *fellow. Not, as foolishly supposed, from* Lord Dane, *but from* lourdin *or* falourdin, *French.*

Lordyngys, &c., *sirs, masters, gentlemen.*

Lore, *doctrine.*

Lough, *laugh, laughed.*

Loves. *Of all loves, an adjuration frequently used by Shakspeare and contemporary writers.*

Low, *laughed.*

Lowde and stylle, *windy and calm ; foul and fair; i.e. in all seasons ; at all times.*

Lowhe, *laughed.*

Lowsed, *let go, let fly.*

Lust, *desire, inclination.*

Lyghtly, &c., lyghtlye, *quickly, nimbly.*

Lynde. *See* linde.

Lyst, *inclination, desire.*

Lystenyth, *listen.*

Lyte, *little.*

Lyue, *life.*

Masers, *drinking cups.*

Maugre, *in spite of.*

Maugref, mawgrefe,*ill-will.*

Maystry. *More maystry, something in a more masterly or capital stile ; a still cleverer thing.*

Mede, meed, *reward.*

Menyvere, *a sort of fur.*

Mestoret, *needed.*

Met, *meet, meted, measured.*

Metelesse, *meatless, without meat.*

Meyny, *assembly, multitude.*

Mo, *more.*

Mote, *might ; may.*

Mought, *might.*

Myrthes, *pleasant passages, merry adventures.*

Nar, *nor, than.*

Nete, *cows, horned cattle.*

Neys, *nice, fine.*

Nones, *occasion.*

Nowchys of golde, *ornaments for a woman's dress; but not certain whether necklaces or hair pins.*

Nygromancere, *necromancer.*

Offycyal, &c., *the commissary or judge of a bishop's court.*

On dedyn, *undid, untyed.*

On lyue, *alive.*

Oon. *Not at oon, not at one, not friends.*

Ordynaunce, *enjoined or regular practice.*

Other, *either.*

Out horne, *summoning horn, horn blown (as if to arms) in time of danger.*

Paramour, paramowre, *mistress, concubine.*

Parand. His parand and his heir, *his heir apparent.* My heir and parand, *my heir apparent.*

Pay, *satisfaction.*

Pees, *peace, pardon.*

Perry, *jewels, precious stones.*

Plyght, *pledge, give.*

Plyzt, *plight, condition.*

Prece, inprece, *in a press, in a croud, in a throng.*

Preced, *pressed, thronged; pressed forward.*

Preker, *rider.*

Prekyd, *rode up; rode.*

Prestly, *readyly, quickly.*

Preue, *prove.*

Pryme, *morning;* "*The first quarter of the artificial day.*" (TYRWHITT.)

Pyne, *pain, torment.*

Quarel, *cause, suit.*

Quest, *inquest, jury.*

Quod, *quoth, said.*

Quyte, *quit, pay, discharge.*

Rech, *reck, care for.*

Rede, *advice, counsel; advise.*

Remewe, *remove.*

Renne, *run.*

Reresoperys, *after-suppers.*

Rewth, *ruth, pity.*

Rode, rood, *cross.*

Ryall, *royal, magnificent.*

Rysed, *raised, caused to rise.*

Saffe, *save.*

Safurs, *sapphires.*

Same. All in same.

Saye, *saw.*

Sayne, *say.*

Schrewe, *shrew, wicked or cursed one.*

Scredely, *shrewdly.*

Se, *seen; see, regard, superintend, keep in sight.*

Sen, *since.*

Sesse. Feffe and sesse, *enfeof and seise,* sub. *in house or land.*

Sheene.

Shent. Make officers shent, *cause them to be reprimanded.*

Shete, *shoot.*

Shot window, *a window that opens and shuts.*

Shrewe, *wicked or cursed one.*

Slawe, *slain.*

Smotley, *pleasantly.*

Sompnere, *summoner or apparitor; an officer who serves the summonses or citations of the spiritual court. See Chaucer's* Canterbury Tales.

Sothe, *truth.*

Sowne, *sound.*

Soyt, *soth, sooth, truth.*

Sper, spyrre, *ask, enquire.*
Spercles, *sparks (of fire).*
Spycerè, *spices.*
State, *estate.*
Stere, *steer, rule, govern.*
Sterte, *started, flew.* Sterte in the waye, *started, rushed hastily, flew into the street.*
Store, *strong; value.*
Stound, *hour, time.*
Stowre, *fight.*
Stynte, *stay.*
Suspitious, *significant.*
Sweythyli, *swiftly.*
Syke, *sigh.*
Syth, *since.*
Tan, *taken.*
Tane, *take.*
Teene, *grief, sorrow.*
Tempre, *correct, manage.*
Tent, *heed.*
The, *thrive.*
Tho, *then.*
Throng, *ran.*
To, *two.*
Trate, *trot, hag.*
Trew mannys lyfe, *the life of an honest man.*
Trewe man, *honest man.*
Tyrsty, *trusty.*
Undurnome, *taken up, received, or entertained (as a notion).*
Undurzode, *understood.*
Unnethes, *scarcely.*
Verament, *truly.*
Villany, *mischief, injury.*
Vowsed.
Voyded, *avoided, withdrew, made off, got out of the way.*

Vylany, *mischief, injury.*
Vyleus, *vile, villainous, shameful.*
Waran, *warn.*
Ware, *expend, lay out.*
Ware, *purchase.*
Warne, *prevent, hinder.*
Wede, *coat, cloak, dress, attire, clothing.*
Weke. Thy furst weke, *at thy first waking; as soon as thou wakest.*
Wend, *go.*
Wende, *weened, thought.*
Were.
Wet, wete, *know.* .
Wight, *strong.*
Wis, *think, take it.*
Wode, *mad.*
Wone, *hesitation.*
Wood, *mad.*
Wost, *wotest, knowest.*
Wreste, *turn.* Wreste it all amysse; *turn it the wrong way: a metaphor from tuning the harp.*
Wreth.
Wyght, *strong.*
Wyle, *feint, device, trick.*
Wynde, *wend, go.*
Wynke, *sleep.*
Wynne, *earn, get; get, come.*
Wyrche, *work, conduct thyself.*
Wys, *trow, think.*
Wyste, *knew, was aware.*
Wyt, *know.*
Wyte, *blame.*
Wytt, *know.* Do the wele to wytt, *let thee perfectly know.*

Y, &c., *I.*
Y do, *done.*
Yede, *went.*
Yeffe, *if.*
Yeffor, *ever.*
Yong men, yonge men, *Yeomen.* *See* Spelmanni Glossarium, vv. Juniores, Yeoman.

Yslaw, *slain.*
Ywys, *I trow, I know.*
Zarn, *yarn.*
Ze, *ye.*
Zerde, *rod.*
Zere, *years.*
Zeyr day.
Zonge, *young.*
Zyt, *yet.*

www.ingramcontent.com/pod-product-compliance
Lightning Source LLC
Chambersburg PA
CBHW021527270326
41930CB00008B/1123